MAKING ARRANGEMENTS

For Mike —

with best
wishes —

Matt

3 . 6 . 82

Also by Matt Simpson

Letters to Berlin (Driftwood Publications, 1971)
A Skye Sequence (Driftwood Publications, 1972)
Watercolour from an Approved School (Toulouse Press, 1975)
Uneasy Vespers (The Windows Project, 1977)

MAKING
ARRANGEMENTS

Matt Simpson

BLOODAXE BOOKS

ISBN: 0 906427 40 1

First published 1982 by
Bloodaxe Books
P.O. Box 1SN
Newcastle upon Tyne NE99 1SN

The publisher acknowledges the financial assistance
of Northern Arts.

Typesetting & cover printing by
Tyneside Free Press Workshop Ltd, Newcastle upon Tyne.

Printed in Great Britain by
Unwin Brothers Ltd, Old Woking, Surrey.

For Norman Nicholson

Acknowledgements

Acknowledgements are due to the editors of the following publications in which some of these poems have appeared: *Critical Quarterly*, *Divan*, *The Fitzwilliam Magazine*, *Lancashire Life*, *The Literary Review*, *New Poetry 2* (Arts Council, 1976), *The New Review*, *Outposts*, *Phoenix*, *P.M.*, *PN Review*, *Poetry Review*, *Quarto*, *Smoke*, and *The Times Literary Supplement*.

Some of them have been broadcast by BBC Radio Merseyside and by Radio City.

'Peer Group', 'Away from It All', and 'Song of Caedmon' appeared in the pamphlet *Watercolour from an Approved School* (Toulouse Press, 1975).

Contents

'Every man thinks meanly of himself for not having been a soldier, or not having been at sea.'
– Samuel Johnson

My Grandmother's African Grey

My father's brother brought it home,
madcap Cliff, a 'case', with wit as wild
as erotic dreams. It was his proof
of Africa and emblem of the family pride
in seamanship.
                    But the parrot quickly sensed
our pride was ragged. Perverse, it
nipped its feathers out
with tar-black pincering beak, until,
baring a stubbly breast, it looked
like poultry obscenely undead.

A gift to grandma and to Auntie Bell
who lived together, two odd shoes
inside a wardrobe of a house, it learnt
to parody my grandma's Liverpudlian
wash-house talk, her lovely common-
as-muck, which it counterpointed faithfully
with Auntie Bell's posh how-d'you-do's
that froze you to politeness:
Sunday Best, with little finger cocked.

The bird survived them both, lost all sense
of Africa, one quarter of a century on a perch.
Shabby slate-grey feathers came to mean
my grandmother; its tail's red splash
was Auntie Bell—their stout and brandy accents
jangling on inside the cage.

To Tom in Canada

His skin was bruised like windfall fruit,
bronchitis rattled at his throat. I should
have written then—discovering him, your father,
destitute like that; but shock's a thing
the heart will hoard.

              The visit was
disguised, a casual calling-in, our
annual fixture of surprise. No longer
belonging, we looked official, parked
in the old-rope grey of that cold street.

Where there'd be
warm welcoming again I steered
my daughter to a house I'd once
learnt love in, for her to attest to certainties
that congregate along the years,
                    expecting him
not much more altered than that owlish clock
which sanctioned all the house contained.

The clock still swings its pendulum.
But he is dead; and you,
leaping the Atlantic to a father's grave
that neatly, quickly closed on him,
have come and gone.

In one short afternoon we blankly stared
together at the estuary, across the beach
with all its mob of ghostly gulls, where once
we'd towed daft girls and swivelled foot-
marks in damp sand, sceptically interpreting
our fathers' war, watching their concrete pyramids
sink, emplacements fill with sand and flies.
Then back to streets with poets' names
which now fall to another blitz.

We are
an age when deaths begin to tell on us,
queueing up to test our nerve. Love does this
to all of us. As we walked the Esplanade,
did you feel it sharpening?

Who's Who in Bootle
(for Philip Gardner)

Whoever named the streets where I grew up,
he must have been a simple-minded philanthrope
who wished brave things on Working Men,
or some at-a-loss committee man
who knew a bright librarian.

A grand eccentric pantheon
of poets and of novelists was where I lived,
illustrious names that no-one knew
and some, like Cow-per, mispronounced.

Dryden, Pope, and Akenside,
Prior, Smollett, Bowles, and Keats.
But who the hell was Falconer? And who
were Beattie, Armstrong?   Eliot, of course,
was only George. And now I know
who Bulwer was (where our house stood):
a dandy lord who wrote of Pompeii's Last Days.
He should have been here for the Blitz.

The curfew tolled at Gray Street school
each nine a.m.; but the Gray was adjectival.
And Norton Street—I suppose the one of *Gorboduc*
(but where was Sackville?)—saw the start
of my romances and cute eventual tragedies
with choirgirls from St Leonard's Church.

It was under a lamp in Prior Street
that poets started mattering (like sex).
From a library book my Best Friend read
a wanton and corrupting thing:
'Or . . . through the paddler's bowl/Sailed up the sun.'
It sounded wild iambic gongs across grey roofs.
And Tennyson, Waller, Kipling, and Scott,
Moore, and Gower, and all the rest,
like Rip Van Winkles, rubbed their eyes.

The Last Days of Pompeii

*'The story of explosive human passions in the
shadow of an awakening volcano . . . 391 pages.'*

I ought to read it, having been
brought up in Bulwer Street.

Edward Lytton Bulwer, afterwards
Lord Lytton (1803-73), that
'hummiest of bugs'—the Book Club
can't know that he,
in my father's gross codologies,
my boyhood's weekend dandyism
of gaudy tie and cultured quiff,
is family too.

I ought to show more loyalty.

And there's another link to make
this dusty grammar of disaster mine:
flattened, burnt by bombs, our street
has claims on dignity. I too
heard rumblings in the night.

Now after all these years of poetry
I sit with books in Boundary Drive,
weighing up Sir Walter Scott's cold words
on Bulwer's 'slang tone of morality'
and Queenie's labelling him the first
of modern best-sellers.

Remembering too
how in his final landlocked weeks
my dying father asked
for 'reading books' and I had said
I'd nothing that he'd like.

Homecoming

Due on the tide, my father's rusted hulk,
weary from landings at Sicily, sailed
into blitzed Liverpool under the waving swords
of searchlights, into the flash and batter of
the ack-ack guns. Under a sky in panic,
into the erupting port, up-river he came
urging home his helpless and unspeaking love.

Next morning, docked, he slung his canvas bag
about his shoulders like a drunken mate, himself
unsteady in the smoking, settling air, and walked
into our street, turning the corner by
the foundry. The street was flattened—brick and wood
in scorched disorder. 'I thought that you were goners,'
he afterwards said, finding us safe up-town
at my grandma's house.

And I remember the last few days,
the quivering run-up hours to that street's death:
a five-year-old and his mother hunched
under the stairs, with the fat chrome springs
of an obsolete pram jigging over my head
and plaster puffing white dust in our hair,
the sky droning and tingling blasts
as a neighbouring street went down.

'We moved that day,' my mother used to say,
'and that same night your dad came home.'
She prized the weird coincidence. It was
as if someone had given her flowers.

Studio Portrait

My sepia great-grandmother
stares out from time
before my time—a time
ingenuous with flowers
and solid parlour furniture,
spindle-legged, high-backed,
as if someone's
just wheeled her in to do
an Old Ma Riley party piece
she will decline uncertainly.

To think of fear so decorous,
so buttoned up. Her only flesh
is head and hands
and head is level with those flowers
a dicky-birding man intends
as obvious analogy.
At her throat
like a trained beetle squats
a cameo brooch. And hands
display with rings
connections and fidelities.
And eyes are swift and vivid with
disasters—splintering rope,
the plunging down through holds,
the barely understood
gunning down in No Man's Land.

This face I could have kissed.
Not that wax
my mother held me up to see
in a room
they'd blinded out the daylight from
in a time
that had already started to
be mine. And death's.

Hospital Visit

My mother's mother, eighty-five.
Her hair like cotton-wool fluffed-out,
her face a smear. Only her eyes
(since nothing ever wipes off eyes)
definite, black with beautiful rage.

Twice in half-an-hour they seemed
to find my face. 'Matt, it's Matt,'
I urged. But she'd gone back
to glaring: something impatient
prowled the ward, some carrion-
monger she had to watch.

At the bedside, too, an aunt not seen
for thirteen years. 'Not since
your mother's death,' she said,
intent on estimating love.

And Cousin Marge, her daughter, still
searching me for la-di-dah,
reviving rites of sarcasm.

Three of us untrained
in watching out for death,
attentive to those glaring eyes,
the all-that-was-left of what we knew,
and anxious to woo back
something to chide our fear.

I drove home to a room
rigid with objects. It was as if
a retrospective exhibition had been staged
of what my life contained. My things
disowning me, just waiting
for purchasers to collect.

Links with the New World
(for Liverpool's Maritime Museum)

They never shipped slaves here, except
odd ones to valet horses or to bring white cards
on silver trays to where fastidious women sat.
And yet spliced in with Mersey's scent of brine
and oil you sometimes smell black sweat
or hear (old seamen awed me with this yarn)
from pavements, oozing out, dark groans
under gratings near the waterfront;
or from the bellies of tethered cargo boats
faintly, but distinctly, catch
a babble of evolving blues. You can inspect
in the extant deck plans of old ships
that tangled masts at Liverpool
the merchants' callous symmetries,
resembling hobnails in a boot,
apportioning breathing space to slaves
swapped for sugar, cotton—moulting bales
trundled through damp Lancashire.

                                          Now
into rundown Georgian terraces
those slaves have sent disconsolate ghosts
chafing for room. The city's sullen conscience
walks common paving stones.

Dead Carthorse on the Shore

Food is the dead we do not recognise
as dead. Prolonged into our lives,
the hacked beast, stripped fowl, drowned fish
inhabit meaning still. But this dead horse
the sea has dumped, that lies
in a depression which the tide
has vacuumed out from round its bulk,
is out of range. I must resort to images
to budge its weight from eye to mind:
a shifting, clattering deck, sprung ropes,
a headlong pitch of life poured out
towards the unhungry sea. Or some
old cocklepicker's drudge, collapsed
between the shafts, abandoned, borne
far down the coastline like a clump
of unhitched seaweed, thrown up here.
Such images do not appease. Something
too solemn for explanation's lodged
hard in the heart, which not even
this powerhouse of flies can chorus out.

Bootle Streets

Salt winds keep these ocean-minded streets
voyaging. There are men here who, landlubbered
(wedded, winded, ulcered out), still walk as if
steel decks were rolling underfoot: riggers
and donkeymen, dockhands and chandlers,
shipwrights and scalers, who service ships
with something of love's habits, insisting on
manhood and sweet memories.

Look in one bedroom. On
the glass-topped dressing table stood
a carved war-painted coconut Aztec head –
to me, memento mori, shrunken thing,
who watched death dredge this bed.
And yet for years it was a trophy,
souvenir of all the thousand miles
of furrowed brine, of fragrant isles.
Consider my mother's photograph beside,
her scissored form revealed against
a satin ground of South American butterflies,
wings of phosphorescent blue,
of tropic midnight, bluer than any sky
that ever settled round these roofs.

My father's second, widowed wife
lies in that bed remembering
holidays in Spain, while I
the other end of the city build,
from images of boyhood, paper boats.

My Father's Father

A shipping baron, high-collared and cravat,
with high ceilings in Rodney Street
and my grandmother in service, down
upon her knees.
                    Ledger script,
a best-behaviour copperplate,
red morocco desk top and gilt frames
of chestnut mares and clipper ships.

'In service' is the only part that's true,
prised out of tight-lipped aunts; the rest's
a daftness from the smell of brine
that's in my nostrils all the time.

My father was a stowaway who never knew
who it was that tucked him in the hold.

Sometimes I wonder at our name,
the fiction I inhabit and hand on,
and wish for my inheritance of fact.
Something signed would be enough.

Crazy Paving

Straddling cracks, each foot on an island,
the small boy, bewildered, sulks down at his shoes,
brand-new and blue as the all-clear sky.
He is not grateful the war is over.
Look up, smile, someone is bullying.

Later they snap his home-from-sea father,
scraping the leavings of milk-rice and nutmeg,
playing the softie, licking the spoon.

The boy has retreated into the house.
It smells of bird seed, peelings and slops.
The draining-board's scrubbed soft as a moth.

Outside there's laughter.
But where are the bluebirds? Is this tomorrow
when the world's free?

North Park

Uncle Walter kept it trim, a corner of
the park he 'had the upkeep of':
flower beds and bowling greens perfected by
the rain and his deft razoring, a man
gentled by flowers. The rest
was treeless waste no-one reclaimed
after the Blitz: empty pond and paddling pool
and stretches of old scraggy grass
and cindered hollows where the bright Fair came
under cold rain to trick the town
with 'Jesse James's Bullet Hole'.
Like boys on topmasts, edging round'
the sodden booth, canvas banging in the wind,
we acknowledged death and history:
that film-prop mummy lying there
as chlorine-green as the awful drowned,
the stub mark where the bullet bit.

One Evening after the War

'Sweet Alice Blue Gown' on the radio.
The generations still intact. Not yet known
the news that put my father into bastardy,
stranded in a surname never ours. Not yet
the fracturing deaths that emptied out
the cupboards and the drawers, reduced
a family to its objects, a meagre pile
of misspent love.

                    The song indulged lost grace,
an innocence of grandmothers before Great Wars.
We sat in tense nostalgia; in one
small still moment impressed by love's
impossible possibilities, drawn round
a fire built up to warm a man
due home from wind-scraped docks,
a woman knitting herself to death,
and reddening the cheeks of a boy for whom
her cable stitch was a secret text,
a cuneiform he could not read.

Old Ma Lennon

praised the Lord for Guinness
and people who were good-as-gold.
And all the lines about her face I swore
were never age's but laughter's
perfecting of itself. Perhaps our Bootle
dockland streets conspired to keep
her peasant innocence intact
so someone from them might at least
get into Heaven by a smile.

Now villains, sulky no-goods have the house
that once smelt faintly rancid like an old
and shabby sacristy, where once
her lacquered saints, that watercolour Jesus
tendering simple and exacting love,
were honoured.

If only for her, I would protest
the existence of her Heaven, an eternity
of laughter, smiles; a perpetuity of stout.

Birthday Poem for a Great-Aunt
(November 5th)

'They'll have to shoot me, Matt,' she laughs,
half-ashamed and marvelling, as if
to outlive's a naughtiness she has
excuses for. Today, at eighty-eight,
she'll jig the dust from carpets, flirt
her frock above her knees, outdance me
in gasping.

This is her compliment: to see me still
a hard-faced father's cheeky lad
wanting sixpence and his Sunday lunch.

My memory blurs on worthy things. It's
my teenage daughter who remembers
fires are lit and fireworks go up
on Auntie Sally's day—not me.

So now nudged into it and embarrassed at
how slovenly I get with love, I offer
something at least familiar:

'They'll have to shoot me first.'

Explaining the Death of Uncle

'Caught something in the hospital.' She stared
across the furniture. I had no heart
to contradict. The deep-stained wood,
the balding plush said let it go.

'A good man, Matt.' And I could not deny
the gentleness, his foreign Cockney playfulness.
The furniture required me not to lie. It knew
enough of love to put me in my place.

Same walnut clock, the cake-stand never used
for cakes, that curious poker and the radio
with fretwork cabinet he'd made away at sea –
all knew I'd ducked the funeral.

Family

Some nights, late,
he wobbled home from work
in oilskins streaming rain,
his soaked cap limp,
on a bike that bounced
the dockroad cobbles,
                    bevvied up
and in the mood
for striking out
at all the grim estrangements
in his life:
            an ulcer
brought home with his conscience
from the war which banished him
from ships that steamed beyond
the river mouth, dragging smoke
below the fixed horizon
into other worlds;
                  a wife
whose proper pieties
would only yield to sentiments
coaxed out of him which he,
before and afterwards, despised;
                    and me
the son she knitted with a vengeance for.

And yet at weekends
we were Family. Keen-eyed streets
confirmed him Master when
he led us out to cinemas
or relatives—a dandy
double-breasted man,
raffish in trilby like George Raft,
he looked
that cut-above-the-rest
they knew his wife to be
but puzzled over in the son
who wore a treachery,
the impudence of knowledge in his eyes.

Home from Home

Home (ten miles from home)
is somewhere driven through
tuned in to music, watching the road.

On the left: St Leonard's Church.
I've travelled more than twenty years
from that once blitzed and rebuilt
focus, where all sermon long
I invested choirgirls with
too-intricate psychologies.

Yet theirs the first held-hands
in darks of terraced streets
and urged through flickering dreams
in back-row plush
of local palaces.

Church and cinema sneaked me away
from home, its smell
of oil and rope, of vinegar,
of chastely laundered sheets.

I wonder where in the world's warren
they are and which one's death
would make a sudden hole in me,
whose emigrating not surprise,
or who, like me, feels super-
annuated by teenage kids
and nibbles away a mortgage,
and whose divorce would put
a renegade if-only in my thoughts.

Education, also, exalted and betrayed.
I was the sailor's son who never put to sea.
I left the city like
the Cunard liners and returned
to find their red and black
familiar funnels gone from gaps
between the houses where I'd lived,

those girls become as vulgar as
tattoos along my father's arms.

Peer Group

A saga world. Legal wrangles in the street,
dust-bin shields, split heads,
bonfire raids and debris feuds.

Darkness fell on it. A final dusk
gathering us to ordered homes.

Except our leaders. They were cursed
to live the hard-knock legend out.

Wife-beaters, wrestlers, drunkards, thieves,
they kept the rules, maintained the style,
in spite of blackboards, rulers, canes.

As big as lorries, five proud sons·
who took the road their father took,

boxed, joined the parachute brigade,
stole crates of whiskey from the docks,
did time, and kept my boyhood whole
as something I betrayed
by growing out of, sailing out of sight.

Latin Master

'Thou didst betray me to a lingring book,
And wrap me in a gown.'

With detentions, impositions, cuffs,
he practised his imperial rule
on 'idlers', occupying minds
with legions of the strictest words
footslogged into Liverpool
on a bellyful of ancient deaths.

He altered all our history,
until the sea
seemed to lose its dragging power
and we learnt to hate our dockland streets
and know ourselves barbarian.

His Latin verbs put me to work
inside the fort,
made turncoat of me in the end.

Even his kindness after four o'clock
when he cranked a wind-up gramophone
inviting in his blue-eyed boys
to share the spoils
of Bach cantatas, symphonies by Brahms,
lost us our purchase on the things of home,
made traitors of us to our kind.

Joe Ellis, English Teacher

In a scrag-end classroom, jerry-built
after the War, Joe Ellis chalked
the dirty bits from Shakespeare up
while lorries trundled to drab docks
down Balliol Road. We learnt to grin
the other side of poetry.
                              A man
no-one dared bowdlerise, he taught us
drunk, chain-smoked, and swore:
our respectable headmaster was
'that Belgian bastard', popinjay
and martinet; and looking Meanings up
(like 'popinjay' and 'martinet')
meant taking out our 'big red dics'.

He gave us poetry
like giving away his last half-crown
because it was good to give away.

After his death
some words shook loose:
we heard of years of broken marriage,
of the son she'd kept away from him,
how cancer scorched his body in the end.
It helped to explain his mischief,
his grip on words he loved,
his grip on love itself.

The Ghost of My Mother

What of her history when all the traces
are of him: his hairs bunched in the nose,
the excremental wax that clogs my ears,
a moody sea at work in the veins?
Her death alone was memorable,
a blood-burst in the mouth.
She was his victim—much as I
still carting round his blustering ghost
that beat her down. What of her
when I revamp his tantrums
and sudden shamefaced tenderness
that buys back love with promises,
embittered dreams of something good?
Ghosts are rarely charitable.
And now she nudges me,
with frightened, loving eyes.

Rigger's Wife

Winter, always mean
on love, came in
from wind-possessed black wharves,
its muscles tensed
like hawsers taut with ice.
She learnt to expect
its bullying,
to cope, to count
its pennies wrenched
from days as stiff as slate,
fingering them until they took
her body heat and need
to heart,
while cold winds
rattled window-frames
and banged the coal-shed door.

The Other Side of the Street

is a row of faces watching. The windows are
the glad-eyes of the street; the gawping doors
with tongues held back will wag their say
when this is done.

                    They, give them their due,
expect her to be ladylike; but let them bite
on silence for a while:
she will dress, will not be carried down,
an ambulance is indignity enough.

This is like the last of trams, the last
Cunarder facing the horizon. They observe
her exit, marvelling. Each one of them can see
her clutch her handbag to her pain.

Fox Fur

My mother used to shoulder fox.
Dyed black. The brush dripped down
her front like ink.
                        She clipped it
like a bandolier. Snout directed
to her breasts.
                    It frightened me.
More than the brittle corsetry it coiled
round in her upstairs drawer.
                                    Its eyes
were globs of glass, unclosable. Its claws
like nibs. Flat silk belly
the feel of snake. My fingertips
imagined sin.

            Fox,
how many ravenous jumble sales
have they tossed you to
since then?

A Face-Lift

Not the house I knew.
No orange lilies'
flagrant fealty.
No elder bush
stripped for its marshmallow pith
to squeeze between
the finger and the thumb
like a fat bogie.
Something has been traded in.
New sills
a mint-cake white
and pebble-dash as fresh
as apple crumble
now propose another pride
from iron-and-coal's
this house
had settled on.
And this house had
a sense of it.
Blunt wisdoms foundered
long before
workmen levered out
its hob and heart.
Here, knowing that the dreams we use
to coddle us all fail,
my grandmother
knelt down
on her cold kitchen's stone
and in the oven gently plumped
a cushion for her head.

Next-Door's Garden

In summer, grasses
tall and tough as wheat.
She was too old and he, her nephew,
was too dim
for the kind of order gardens need
to look their Sunday Best.

We used to blame our weeds on them:
dandelions, docks,
nudging with peasant clumsiness
our pinks and marigolds aside.
It was sectarian, a rivalry
of roots. We knew she kept
their dingy rooms
plain at saints' behests
to keep a faith with martyrdoms.

Those grasses aimed their seeds
at where our orange lilies grew;
their thistles landed on our lawns,
lodged in the seams of paving stones
my father laid. And efforts
of tidiness, our symmetries,
now faded into tolerance
as I have grown through deaths,
were mocked by their wild garden's
over-populating seed.

And that corridor of trodden path
that went beneath her washing line
was via dolorosa,
where she amid the alien grass
was Mater Mysteria attending
the depositions of shirts.

Bonfire Night and Mr Ellison

On the bombed side of the street,
before they plonked those shoe-box prefabs down,
we raised our bonfire, roofing it
with planks we'd nicked from Barney's Yard.
And when night came and we were still
awake in all its wickedness,
we prodded rolled newspaper torches in
between the planks to let the fire rip.

But in the awe of it, the hush,
we heard the Elloes' drunken father curse
and clatter like a one-man-band
along the street. And next,
the pistol shot of a slammed front door,
his whingeing wife,
thin as a needle, quick as a pain,
dragging off four yapping dogs of sons
around the foundry corner
and away up Knowsley Road.

No-one called me in. I was left
with a bonfire playing merry hell
with the dark, while half-seas Mr Ellison,
tottering like a bull come round
from surgery, hauled out and flung
curtains, chairs, and table legs
among the splintering flames. And moved
by generosity: 'There's something
for your bommy, Matt.'

Finally the sideboard's bulk.
But halfway across the cobbled street
strength and fury failed. 'I'll have
a bloody bommy by meself,' he said,
striking matches into drawers.

Just two of us, alone, with darkness winning:
me not twelve years old, and him
slumped on the kerbstones, blubbering.

Blossom Street

Memories and places. A jumbled itinerary
of journeying undergone.
                              It is myself
I am compiling, re-arranging a town
for reasons I don't understand.

Yesterday I parked, pulled in across
a residue of snow and walked
around the corner to a shop I'd found
last year—student cast-offs, books
in clumsy piles.
                    What is it that
accuses? I walked the length
of Blossom Street,
                        caught by a name
from thirty years ago, a terraced street,
ancestral place I'd never seen before.

But from here my father as a boy
was off-loaded to a Training Ship.
This is where the gibings start.
From here his ruined boyhood comes
spilling into what I have become.
This is where the sea begins its mutterings.

The place a memory, the memory a place.

The Beautiful Woman

She hasn't smiled, all evening
hasn't once betrayed
whatever sadness she's intent upon.
And yet for sure
she's seen a dockside commonness
beneath my skin,
the poet and the lecturer.

We're here to listen to poetry,
to children being dutiful,
handling poems they wrote for me
like jam or flowers at a fête.
She is used to this. Her sad
and beautiful face consents. Is this
an image for breeding's end?
Is she too dying of
a sort of emotional anaemia?

This green county's hers and all
its sky; Land Rover or Volvo shake
its hedges when she drives.
If I envy anything
it's the River Severn running through
her ancient land like a great nuisance.
Among its shimmying streamer weed
chub and barbel tensely hang;
and some of them have dropped their poise
to encounter me head-on
through the exact incision of a line.

Old Flame

It was there in her handshake again,
the something known and given up on
twenty years ago. Not softness
which can be tensed with urging but
that old limpness which always seemed
to be saying a vague goodbye.

John Middleton, the Childe of Hale (1578-1623)

The local gentry gaudied me
to bring before the freakish king.
Tobacco, witches he was hot against.
Wrestling though
he liked; and I was prodigy enough.
I earned a purse of twenty pound
for putting out
his champion's thumb.

At Brasenose then
they went about my measurements;
full-length in all my lendings
painted me in oils,
while jackdaw scholars pecked about
my cowpat hands. I told them lies:
that dozing in a sandy place
I woke this size, burst all my clothes
like gorsepods in the summer's heat,
and stepping forth at nine-foot-three
met and hurled a fuming bull
head-first into Mersey silt.

And I was landmark after this
among the clods and fields of Hale.
But still my head undutifully turned
towards the river's runs of gold
each time I saw a sunset pour
its crucible. And sometimes too
the river glistened like a brand-
new knife, gulls threw their wings
like money thrown up carelessly.

It was then I longed
for marvels to be home among,
over the horizon's rim
where tall men walk ungawped-at.

At night I crawled into my mother's house
on hands and knees like some great dog.

Funeral

Winds come sniffling up from the docks,
cold winds smelling of cargoes.
Some of my old selves are walking to meet me,
ganging up to challenge claims
on kinship and love.

                    A spade is offered:
Take and eat: this is her body.
I crumble soil like wet cake.
The Chapel surveys its shipwrecks
through the eyes of a dead clock.

Is this where
the back-tracking finally leads,
to a foetal snugness six feet down?
Sprinkling dirt I seem to make
a reluctant promise to return.

Back at the house
they do not talk of her; they need
to measure distances by praising me.
I'm fed with cake and whiskey pours
to let me know I'm prodigal,
the Scholarship Boy, head stuffed
with perfidious magics, home
for a funeral.

Buried at Sea

He entered the Gulf Stream
as if to ferment it,
give it body and percentage proof
of spirit. And all the briny molecules
rejoiced. Crabs savoured his coming;
polyp and tentacle reached out.
He dissolved in them. The whale's jaw
filtered him; the bivalve belched
its gratitude. The neatest grain
of him was sucked
through membranes of the silkiest cells
that scurry through unending sea. It was
his purest, his most generous act.

'Buried at sea,' my father proudly said
of his Best Man,
recalling berths and watches shared
through years and miles of open sea,
not knowing then
that they would tip his ashes out
in a family plot of rain-soaked land.

Myocardial Infarction

A hammer slipping and a blister
elderberried on the thumb,
a kettle spilt and a burn
fruiting in a mistletoe,
a knee scuffed like a toe-cap,
or neat capillaries red-inked
along the skin by a riled cat's nibs –
and he would say
'It'll be a pig's foot in the morning.'

Things invisible and serious,
dark-rooted pain, an ache that pulsed
the eyeballs—and he'd say 'One more
clean shirt for you, my lad' or 'Time
to dust the policies.'

And now here's me:
a pig's foot in the chest,
the planet-surface of the heart
blipped by meteorites. 'This one's
convicted,' doctors said
with their forever-word.

Part of my heart is dead,
gone gangrenous,
sloughed off and scarred. Do I say
it's strengthened by its scar,
is tougher now?

Statistics are undermining me.
And who's that climbing in the loft,
rummaging for documents,
huffing and puffing?
Who's counting shirts?

Brown's Nautical Almanac, 1934

In this determiner of stars and tides,
ascensions, declinations, azimuths,
of navigable distances, beacons, buoys,
I see my father holding course
for the New World of his marriage,
myself two years away from sliding down
the slipway, dragging chains.

Here are his totems: polished brass
clinometers, liquid compass binnacles,
course correctors, sounding gear.
Here is esoteric lore: ephemeris
for tracking over sea and sky
by star-conjunction, numbered tides.
By this his bearings can be true
for civil days in port.

And here are hoisted storm cones
he must have seen: his rusty cut-wave
by North West Light and Bell Boat Beacon
thrusting in on Liverpool.

Making Arrangements

Look at the map. The streets where I grew up
move in a direction hard to resist,
lines of force that drag down to grey docks,
to where my father spent his strength.

I am making these arrangements into meaning
to re-inhabit after twenty years some places of
myself—backyards full of ships and cranes,
of hard-knock talk, and death—not just
to mouth at ghosts, unless there's welcoming
in such a courtesy; not merely exorcise:
I'd like to talk at this late stage on equal terms,
declare a kind of coming of age
to those who have implanted death in me.

And yet I'm only staring into empty drawers
and cupboards where a sediment of dust has dropped
on papers with dead dates and on events
in a world that looks naïver than my own.

The streets drag down to docks—to warehouses,
derricks, pigeons, and hard men
that I resisted twenty years ago
by riding inland, choosing softer options
they would say.

                    I think perhaps
it's time to gauge whatever love
there was or might have been, or time
to ask the dead to let me estimate
their suffering by the yardstick of my flesh,
time at last to come home to myself.

Ashes to Ashes

A gate closed, a gate between privets
palsied with soot. The breath
went out of the house.

Six feet of path,
two squares of soil
where flowers put on
brave faces for the street,
a doorstep scrubbed and holystoned,
four rooms oppressed by furniture,
a banked-up fire that smouldered with
intensities
of Father, Mother, Only Child.

Two dead:
a strong slow violence taking both
eight years apart. The same
green-distempered hospital, the same
bleak comforts at the crematorium,
the same rain falling.

And not much to show:
two bagfuls of ash we scattered on
the family plot,

                    as if to fertilise,
as if a red rose and a briar should grow
to blazon all the violence again.

Seaforth Shore Revisited

A vague perversity has brought me here
to routine waves. Behind me now
the town that tried to push me out to sea,
into my family's element. And literate,
I've puzzled out new roads,
roundabouts, flyovers, to come to this
old tramping-ground of clinkered sand
and fifty visible miles of sea,

forgetting how much sky
included me.

A gawky know-all girl avowed
that Turner painted sunsets here
dipping his brush in the raging fires
that slither into Ireland. And Sassoon
tossed his medal in this sea's grey face
glaring across the estuary to where
Wilfred Owen chased the winds
on horseback on New Brighton sands
before that war which trampled them.
And here we rummaged in the sand
for skulls and shrapnel,
scavenging like gulls to prove
our war.

Behind, behind for good,
the town's indifference. The rubble of
my toppled street is long bulldozed away.
Only sea and sky renew the thought
of freedoms brighter than my father hoped
wishing me to take his turn
over that horizon there.

Ferry Crossing
(for Catherine)

Ten minutes' seamanship:
up abruptly,
like a fairground ride –

the screws' back-churn
lifting the Mersey under us,
swinging the stern to shore

and bringing us back
to this nervous and emaciated place,
Liverpool, we must call home,

father and daughter,
heads in a wind
smelling of salt—you concerned

to fathom my ghosts, those tough
old tars flying
in our wake,

and in that gull-crazed wind,
in a special effort of love,
you too showing me wings.

Away from It All

Even here the seagulls come. Among the hills
where falcon, buzzard grimly range.
Even in valleys that belong to swifts
and linnets, where a rare kingfisher shoots
along the trout streams like electric charge,
they bring unwelcome white and grey.

Last night it rained, drowned out the owl, and on
the caravan's tin roof a medieval army drummed
itself into ferocious war. I dreamt
the seagulls were all driven back
into the sea.

Nothing so healthy.
Just two at first, perched hard-faced
like officers of some press gang, scurvy birds
with ancient curses on their beaks.

And then all day,
glinting white against green slopes, like words
hovering over blankness, wanting poems.

The Song of Caedmon

And God said:
sing me somewhat, Caedmon.

I would have sung the mullet and whiting
shoaling at Whitby, the occasional porpoise
that breaks a summer horizon, the pigs
and goats poked into market.
I'd have had men listen
to new songs at harp-passings,
sung the wondrous windwork of gulls.

But God thought otherwise, sold me on dreams:
sing me Creation, Caedmon, the song
that's acceptable, that does me some credit.

So I the uneducated
was saddled with miracle; big words
broke on me, a galeforce of syllables
swept up from nowhere. I would have welcomed
a start nearer home, a local beginning.

But God thought otherwise:
work on my handiwork, carve it on crosses,
sing in Northumbrian the way the world got to
this bleak point of history. Sing to the mindful,
make me some worship.

I would have started the other way round,
charting our wonders, the wonders about us,
the disorder of gulls in a pleasure of words,
the glint of the mullet, the pigness of pigs.

Matt Simpson was born in 1936 in Bootle on Merseyside. His family were of sea-going stock, the men finishing their working lives on or around the Liverpool docks, as riggers and warehousemen. He grew up in the streets around Gladstone Dock, went to Bootle Grammar School for Boys, and then read English at Cambridge; he has taught in schools and colleges, and since 1966 has been a lecturer in English at the Liverpool Institute of Higher Education.

Matt Simpson's poems have appeared widely in many magazines and anthologies. He has published four pamphlets. *Making Arrangements* is his first book-length collection.